Mind, Body, Spirit

The Ultimate Guide to Creating a Strong Mind, Body, Spirit Connection

Mind, Body, Spirit

Healthy Body Books

http://www.healthybodybooks.com

ISBN-13:
978-1500960704

ISBN-10:
1500960705

Copyright 2013 by Haven Publishing Group- All rights Reserved

All rights reserved. No part of this book may be reproduced by any mechanical, photographic, or electronic process, or in the form of a phonographic recording; nor may it be stored in a retrieval system, transmitted, or otherwise be copied for public or private use—other than for "fair use" as brief quotations embodied in articles and reviews—without prior written permission of the publisher.

This document is geared towards providing exact and reliable information in regards to the topic and issue covered. The publication is sold with the idea that the publisher is not required to render accounting, officially permitted, or otherwise, qualified services. If advice is necessary, legal or professional, a practiced individual in the profession should be ordered.

The author of this book does not dispense medical advice or prescribe the use of any technique as a form of treatment for physical, emotional, or medical problems without the advice of a physician, either directly or indirectly. The intent of the author is only to offer information of a general nature to help you in your quest for emotional, spiritual and physical well-being. In the event you use any of the information in this book for yourself, which is your constitutional right, the author and the publisher assume no responsibility for your actions. Under no circumstances will any legal responsibility or blame be held against the publisher for any reparation, damages, or monetary loss due to the information herein, either directly or indirectly.

The information herein is offered for informational purposes solely, and is universal as so. The presentation of the information is without contract or any type of guarantee assurance.

The trademarks that are used are without any consent, and the publication of the trademark is without permission or backing by the trademark owner. All trademarks and brands within this book are for clarifying purposes only and are the owned by the owners themselves, not affiliated with this document.

Table Of Contents

Table Of Contents 4

Introduction 5

Keep Up to Date with New Releases 7

Chapter 1 Finding Balance 8

Chapter 2: The Body 11

Chapter 3 The Mind 18

Chapter 4 The Soul 22

Chapter 5 Creating the Connection 24

Steps to Success Action Plan 28

Conclusion 30

Other Books you may be interested in... 31

Free Gift 32

Introduction

Do you feel like you would like to be more balanced?

Do you feel like there is a disconnect in you?

Do you sometimes feel like you are missing something?

Would you like to feel whole, and be the best version of you, you can be?

In this book you will discover the most up-to-date information on connecting your Mind, Body and Spirit for life including:

-How to find Balance

-Connecting the Body

-How to connect to your mind

-Connecting your Spirit

And much more!

I want to thank you and congratulate you for buying this book, "Mind, Body, Spirit: The Ultimate Guide to Creating a Strong Mind, Body, Spirit Connection!"

Taking the first step is sometimes half of the battle!

I would also like to introduce myself; my name is Simone, the creator of the Healthy Body Books. My deep-seated passion for health has driven me to create these books. Something inside of me has always called out, encouraging me to write books that health-minded individuals would want to read. Health has always been a priority in my life, even when a recent change in my routine made it much more difficult to find myself.

In spite of not feeling my best (or even much like myself), I found ways to continue achieving my goals. After searching long and hard, I found that natural therapies, diets and self-help were enough to help me get things back under control. I found out that these natural remedies were doing so much for me – and I never looked back.

If you are trying to find another way to stay healthy, the Healthy Body Books are for you. If you are anything like me, you might need to find an alternative method to reach your peak. Written by experts in terms that anybody can read, these books are designed to help you identify which aspects of your life just do not seem to be working for you. You should not let anything stop you from being the person you want to be – or from living the life you want to live. This book will help you along you journey.

Good luck!

Keep Up to Date with New Releases

Thank you again for grabbing yourself a copy of this Book Mind, Body, Spirit: The Ultimate Guide to Creating a Strong Mind, Body, Spirit Connection

I'd like to offer you the chance to stay up-to date on new books with free access to my newsletter!

You will be getting up to date information on health, fitness and diet, and also get access to getting other Healthy Body Books for free. By joining my newsletter you will be taking a big step forward in being your Healthiest Body yet!

Just visit http://www.healthybodybooks.com and get free instant access to the Healthy Body Books newsletter today!

Chapter 1 Finding Balance

Throughout history, different views about the mind, body, and spirit have been given. Many philosophers had stated various theories regarding the individuality and interconnectedness of these three entities. Renowned Greek Philosophers Plato and Aristotle were among the first to share their views regarding this matter.

Plato, in his Theory of Forms, concluded that whatever it is that you perceive in this world are mere shadows and that the Forms neither exist physically nor mentally. This theory was found to be ambiguous and so Aristotle formulated his own doctrine. In his theory, Aristotle pointed out the potential of the body, which he called the matter, to change and the ability of the humans to comprehend, reflect and reason, which he thought to be due to the soul. More studies of the soul were done by Saint Thomas Aquinas where he said that the soul is the substance that makes up every person. His theory strengthened Aristotle's doctrine that a human being is made up of two principles: the form and the matter with the former pertaining to the soul and the latter to the body.

This mind-body unifying principle was later on contrasted by Rene Descartes who claimed that the mind and the body could exist separately. He called the mind the "thinking being" while the body the "material substance." Though Rene Descartes' Theory of Dualism claims that the mind and body are two separate entities, it also claims that there is some degree of interaction between the two. However, how the interaction occurs can only be explained by various theories and this created the "Mind-Body Problem" or the "Problem of Interactionism."

MIND, BODY, SPIRIT

Up to the present day, people still search for the link that binds the mind, body, and spirit. Can the mind truly affect the body and soul? How does it happen? The body is said to be the tool that links the mind and the external environment, while the mind is responsible for one's judgment, intellectual function, insight and perception. On the other hand, the soul is said to be inner driving force of a human being.

History and personal experiences have proven mankind that a strong association among these three dimensions exists and that one cannot function without the other. However, most people would only focus on one aspect, which is more often than not, the body. One example of this scenario is the rising incidence of mental illnesses. People who are having trouble with their thought content and thought processes, like those who are having hallucinations or depressive episodes, do not seek help immediately. This differs greatly to a person's response to a physical illness. A simple back pain, cough or headache is enough reason for a person to go to the emergency department.

The soul is another aspect of the human being that has been forgotten and ignored. The soul gives the person the strength to go on with his life, the motivation to fulfill his dreams, and the reason to act appropriately. However, in this day and age, most people only act according to what they feel and think; not according to what they believe and desire.

Because of the misconception that the body is more important than the mind and the soul, a widening disparity between these three aspects develops. The gap that it has creates can lead to disintegration of human values, performance of unreasonable actions, and development of diseases. It is thus essential to find the balance and connection among these three dimensions.

Balance can only be attained if all the three entities are healthy, which means that they are able to perform their functions and fight off stressors without being ruined in the process.

Chapter 2: The Body

The body has long been known as the temple of the spirit and because of that, it has to be protected, respected, and taken care of. The body is so special because it is the only medium of contact of the spirit to the outside world. It is the bridge that connects you to the environment, a link that helps you interact with other people, and the vehicle that helps your mind and soul grow.

The body must be kept healthy at all times because it is the agent that helps you achieve your dreams, the tool that you use for your survival and the medium that nourishes your mind and soul. You navigate through your eyes, you eat through your mouth and hands, you hunt with your feet and you breathe through your nose. Without the body, the mind and soul cannot exist.

Despite the fact that the body is a sacred tool, people always take advantage of it. Use of vices like smoking, drinking too much alcohol to the point of intoxication, and others, is a sign of disrespect to one's body. Stress and work are also factors that can lead to physical imbalance, which can only be avoided and managed with proper diet, exercise and right amount of sleep.

1. Proper Diet

Since childhood, you have been taught about the importance of a balanced diet. You have learned how yellow and orange vegetables can improve eyesight, how red meat can prevent iron deficiency anemia, and how fiber-rich foods can improve bowel motility and elimination. The question here is, "How can you get or absorb as much nutrient as you can from these foods?" Surely, each fruit, vegetable and meat is overflowing with minerals and vitamins, but sometimes, improper preparation of these foods can lead to the loss of nutrients.

Eat fresh. One of the best ways to extract the minerals and vitamins from food is to eat them fresh or raw. Fruits must be freshly-picked, while vegetables must be newly-harvested, and meats must not be stored for long periods of time. The fresher they are, the more minerals and vitamins you can get. The same is true when you eat them raw. Nutrients get lost in the process of cooking these foods, thus, are better eaten when raw. Vitamins like Vitamin C and A are unstable vitamins, which means that they easily get degraded with extremes of temperature. Vegetables and fruits containing these vitamins must only be half-cooked to prevent total loss. When boiling these vegetables, don't discard the broth.

Proper food preparation and storage. As mentioned earlier, there are unstable vitamins and minerals that are lost as the food is cooked or prepared. Fruits like apples and bananas turn darker when exposed to air. This is because of the reaction of the different chemicals in the food and the components of air that can acidify the fruit. To prevent acidification and consequent nutrient degradation, one must properly prepare and store them. If you need to use these fruits as ingredients, you must slice them right before using them. For the pieces that have to be stored, they must be placed in an air-tight container or covered with Cling Wraps.

Drink 8 to 10 glasses of water every day. Though water does not contain any vitamin or mineral, water is considered to be one of the most basic needs of man. Sixty percent of the body is composed of water and any alteration in the levels of fluid will cause disease. The fluid, in conjunction with the blood, is the body's medium for delivering the nutrients from the gastrointestinal tract to the different parts of the body. It is also the vehicle for transport of waste products from the cells to the organs of excretion, such as the kidneys and intestines. Water is also needed by the cells to keep their shape and functions. Water loss can lead to shrinkage and death of cells. Keep in mind that you can live for two weeks without food, but you can only live for 3 days without water.

Avoid processed foods. In this day and age, almost all of the foods that you can buy in the market have already been processed. Though processing of foods is absolutely beneficial for manufacturing companies, it is not at all beneficial for you. Processed foods contain a lot of chemicals that, when taken in excess, can lead to disease. An example of this is sodium. Most processed foods, especially cured meats, contain high amounts of sodium. Though this mineral is also needed by the body, too much of it can lead to hypertension. Other chemicals present in processed foods include nitrosamines, which are very toxic to cells and can cause cancer. Processing of foods can also lead to nutrient loss because some processing methods require that the food be exposed to extremes of temperature.

Eat slowly. All the foods that you eat must be broken down into small pieces before absorption occurs. By eating slowly and by chewing the food properly, you are helping your stomach digest the food and your intestines to absorb it. According to the experts, the food must be chewed 20 or more times before swallowing to allow the enzymes in the saliva to effectively exert their actions on the nutrients present in the food. Eating slowly can also help you lose weight because it can give you the feeling of early satiety.

Have small frequent feedings instead of one large meal.

Eating small servings of food every 3 hours does not only aid the stomach in digestion; it also helps in metabolism. The body needs constant supply of nutrients to be able to perform its functions well. One of the hormones involved in the metabolism is insulin, which is responsible for the lowering of blood glucose levels by facilitating cellular uptake. Large meals cause a sharp increase in insulin and may cause metabolic alterations like hypoglycaemia. Small frequent feedings, on the other hand, are more beneficial because it keeps insulin levels constant.

2. Proper Exercise

One of the many factors that contribute to development of diseases is a sedentary lifestyle. One should always include exercise in their daily routine because it has been proven to alleviate and prevent certain diseases, like diabetes mellitus and heart attack. Active exercises can improve blood flow, thus improving the delivery of oxygen and other nutrients to the different parts of the body. The muscles that you use during the exercise can also serve as secondary mechanical pumps that push blood back to the heart, thus maintaining adequate cardiac output. Exercise can also promote the release of the body's endogenous opioid, called endorphins, which improves your sense of well-being.

Do aerobic exercises. This type of exercise generally makes use of your weight-bearing joints, such as knees and hips. Walking and jogging are just some of them. Brisk walking is highly recommended among all age groups and in both genders. 10, 000 steps a day is an effective way of reducing the risk of cardiovascular diseases.

Exercise in moderation. Though exercise is important, it is also vital that you don't exhaust your body of energy. Do exercises in moderation and always have a warm-up. If you were not an athlete and you suddenly thought of running, don't run in full speed on your first attempt. This will just exhaust you and you won't be able to run for another round anymore. Instead, pick up speed gradually. Run for 5 km/hr in your first attempt, then 7 km/hr on the next, and so on. This way, you are not exerting your muscles too much and you are avoiding yourself from being fatigued. Fatigue can only cause more injury than benefits to your muscles. If you decide to exercise in a gym and you are planning to do weight-lifting, start with the least weight that you can carry, and then increase the weight as you go on. Stop increasing the weight when you can no longer flex your muscles.

Induce variety in your routine. Make your exercise as enjoyable as you can. Don't settle for boring routines. Exercise is supposed to make you feel good and alive, and not sleepy. Perform different kinds of exercises for the different parts of your body. Don't just focus on your legs, or your arms or your back. Instead, choose an exercise routine that will involve all of them.

3. Proper Sleeping Habits

Sleep is one of the basic needs that the lack of it can make you irritable, depressed, and sub functional. Every person needs 6 to 7 hours of sleep for optimum performance throughout the day. Sleep does not only make your skin smooth and radiant, but it can also greatly improve your mood. With enough sleep, you have enough energy to move, to work, and to think.

Sleeping also has an effect on the renewal of cells. The cells of the body regenerate every night, usually between 11 pm to 5 am, which is most effective during rest. This means that when you sleep late, like for example at around 12 midnight, you already lost 1 hour of effective cell renewal. What happens when you have ineffective cell renewal? If it were the skin cells, you will have dry and rough skin. If it were the blood cells, you will have defective blood cells that can even lead to a slower blood flow.

Eat light at night. Many people report incidences of "nightmares" after eating a heavy meal right before sleeping. Doctors call this condition acute pancreatitis, pathology of the pancreas characterized by inflammation and enzymatic degradation of pancreatic cells. This condition occurs because the food particles block the opening where pancreatic enzymes are released. Thus, instead of the food being digested, it is the cells of the pancreas that are being digested by the enzymes. Sleeping time is also a time for the body to rest; hence, most body processes shut or slow down during this time. Large meals eaten before sleeping won't be digested as much as during waking hours thus must be avoided.

Sleep in a dark and quiet room. The quality of sleep is more important than the number of sleep hours, and this can be improved if you are sleeping in a dark and silent room. Having a light turned on during sleep can also predispose you to certain cancers, thus is not beneficial.

Don't use your bed for anything else. Your bed is your place of sleep. Using your bed for doing assignments, for eating and for other purposes can make it difficult for you to sleep. Why is this so? This is because when you use your bed for other things, you are associating your bed to them and not to sleep. When you see your bed, what do you want to think of? Do you want to think of work or do you want to think of sleep? When you think of work when you see your bed, definitely, sleeping would be a hard thing to do.

Be comfortable. Comfort is one of the most important things that you have to consider when sleeping. Your sleep would be much better when you are lying down on a soft mattress than sitting down on a chair with your head resting on your desk or lying down on the floor. The place of sleep truly matters so keep your bed free from clutters and covered with the softest sheets.

Chapter 3 The Mind

If the body serves as the bridge between the soul and the outside world, your mind is the link between your body and soul. Your mind serves as the interpreter of your soul of what is going on with and around the body. The mind allows for conscious perception of reality, generates a response towards a sensory stimulus and filters the information that the body and the soul receives. The mind is a powerful component of a human person because it can command the body to do something and it can attract whatever it is that it conceives. An optimistic person can attract positive energies, while the opposite is true for the pessimist.

One of the benefits of the mind, and one of its downside, as well, is that it has the power to think of anything and everything limitlessly. In contrast to the body, which can only perform at a certain extent, the power of the mind is boundless. But the problem with it is that the mind becomes cluttered with unnecessary things. Instead of focusing on the essential ones, the mind gets easily distracted by so many things. When it starts to entertain negative thoughts, the mind starts to lose its peace and calm. Thereby, the mind starts to become flooded and the filtering capability of the mind starts to waver.

The mind has to be clear in order to perform its function of filtering and consequently integrating the information being received by the body and the soul. It has to be at peace and it has to be strong to be able to combat worries and anxiety. The mind works on two principles: the self-awareness and focus. Alterations in these two aspects can lead to imbalance that can later on lead to a disease.

1. Self- Awareness

Self-awareness is one of the major roles of the mind, aside from perception and cognition. It involves identifying your own strengths and weaknesses and doing something to improve on them. It is not simply about knowing what you want to become or who you are right now; it is also about knowing how you would most likely respond to a given situation and how you would turn your weaknesses into strengths. Self-awareness is not an easy task because there are things that other people see about you that you don't. In short, self-awareness is not just all about knowing you; it is also about knowing how other people think of you and what they know about you.

Keep a journal. You can only truly know yourself if you are aware of what you did, why you did it, how you did it and your response to what you did. Keeping a journal is one tedious task, but it is also one helpful tool. When writing your journal, don't just include the things that you did, but also try to write the reasons behind doing so, your emotions, and responses to the act. Did you punish your kid because you want him to learn or because he did not listen to you? Keeping a journal with these details can help you map out your personality. You will also be able to see the pattern of your responses to certain acts, so that when you experience the same thing, you would know what to do and what not to do.

Talk to yourself. Some people may think that talking to oneself is crazy. Well, it could be if you don't know how to handle yourself well. To get to know yourself better, it is helpful to ask yourself some questions about your plans for the future, about what you think of the present, and about what happened to you in the past. Talk to yourself like you are talking to a friend and be honest. You can also remind yourself about what you have learned in the past so that you won't make the same mistake in the future.

Be aware of your image. The truth that you know about yourself may not be the same truth that the other people know about you. While it is true that you should not let yourself be controlled by other people's opinions of you, it is also true that it is helpful know what they think of you. This helps you identify your strengths and weaknesses. If they think of you as someone who is strong and brave, this can improve your self-confidence. On the other hand, if they think of you as someone who is coward, you can think of ways on how you can be a brave person.

2. Focus

Focusing is one of the most difficult things to do. When you focus, you have to forget other things in your surroundings and other things that may be boggling your mind right now. When you say that you have to focus on your career, it means that you have to work harder and you have to follow its rules. When you say you want to lose five kilos in one month, you have to be focused on your diet and exercise. Be watchful of what you are eating and be committed on your meal plan. If your meal plan says that you cannot eat even a single scoop of ice cream and a slice of cake, then you have to resist the temptation and stick to your plan.

When you focus your mind to something, you can achieve what you really want. This is the law of attraction. If you think positively, then positive things can happen. If you think negatively, then negative things can happen. Focusing is devoting one's thoughts, time and effort into something, willing it to happen, and in one way or another, making it happen.

Chapter 4 The Soul

The spirit or the soul is the component of the human person that the people have the least knowledge about. This is the most mysterious dimension of all but is as equally as important as the others. In fact, the spirit is believed to be the force that drives all human actions, the intuition that keeps us free from danger, and the entity that provides enlightenment and wisdom.

The soul, though not much is known about it, is said to be men's divine connection. It is said that the soul is your guide to the deeper meanings of human experiences, which teaches you to learn from your own mistakes and helps you understand why certain things happen the way they do. But the most important of all is that the spirit is capable of healing your wounds, and can make you start anew again.

The soul is in constant battle between love and fear, between forgiveness and hate, and between wisdom and ignorance. The spirit, in order to achieve balance, must learn love instead of fear, breed forgiveness instead of hate, and use wisdom rather than ignorance.

1. Love

Love is one of the most powerful things in the world, and so is fear. Thus, every human person is undergoing a constant battle between these two entities. But the difference between the two is the direction where you'll be taken. When you open your spirit to love, you will find peace and harmony in your body, mind, emotions and soul. Walking towards its path will give you joy, while walking towards the opposite side will give you nothing but pain and sorrow.

2. Forgiveness

Forgiveness, if truth be told, is not something that can easily be given, nor is it something that you can easily ask for. This is because forgiveness is all about letting go of the pain and hate that once filled your heart. When your friend betrays you, you cannot forgive him easily because you want to hold onto the pain that he caused you. The hate that you were feeling then served as your support and forgiving him means that you are already letting that support go. Healing needs forgiveness because when you forgive, your soul starts to open up for more positive things.

3. Wisdom

As one grows old, one becomes wiser. Your own experiences, whether they are happy or sad, and your knowledge all contribute to your wisdom. The lessons that you have learned, whether they are from your own or other's experiences, play an essential role in the development of wisdom. As you become wiser, you become more capable of handling stressors and in overcoming life's challenges.

Chapter 5 Creating the Connection

There are times when you feel like you want to die, when you just want to numb all your pain, when you think of all the negative things that are happening in your life, and when you lose your purpose to live a happy and healthy life. When these happen, you realize that there is something missing in your life or that there is a hole in your chest that grows bigger and bigger as the days go by. This then pushes you to seek for something that can fill up the void that you are feeling in your heart. You party with your friends; you keep yourself busy with work, thinking that these are the answers that you have been searching for. What you don't know is that the answer lies within you and that a moment of silence is all it would take for you to get your life back on the right track.

Now that your mind, body, and soul are in a healthy state, you can build and strengthen the connection among these three entities. Walk the road of understanding and it will lead you to a world of wisdom and peace. Give yourself some time to reflect on what is going on with your life, to recollect on the right and wrong things you have done, and to envision a happy and a successful life in the future.

The connection between the mind and the body has already been scientifically proven with more advanced studies about the brain and its functions. The brain is composed of different lobes that are responsible for various mental functions. Your frontal lobe is responsible for short-term memory and speech production; your occipital lobe, which is located posteriorly, is responsible for vision; the parietal lobe is responsible for the perception of your senses; and the

MIND, BODY, SPIRIT

temporal lobe is responsible for comprehension and long-term memory. Other regions of the brain are responsible for specialized functions, such as breathing, temperature regulation, and appetite.

However, there is more to the mind-body connection than that. Your brain constantly produces a series of thoughts that can influence your actions. Have you ever experienced staying on your bed for one whole day because you thought you were too weak, too tired, and too powerless to do anything? How about surpassing the obstacles that you had encountered in your life because you thought you can? These are just examples of how your mind controls your body but if the mind gets out of hand, this tie can be severed.

Your soul, though usually ignored by many people, is also connected to your body. Butterflies in the stomach, gut feeling, instinctual drives - though these things have long been recognized by people as legitimate reasons to do something, the truth about their origin has been unclear until recently when these are said to be proofs that your soul is truly linked to your body.

Yes, it is true that your mind can affect your body and soul, and your soul can affect both your mind and body. The real question here is, "How will you create the connection and strengthen it?" Here are some ways on how you can establish the mind, body and soul connection and how you can use this connection in your everyday life.

1. Meditate

Meditation is now being used as a form of relaxation. However, meditation has been traditionally used as a way of strengthening the connection between your mind, body and soul. Meditation allows you to delve deeper into your consciousness and permits your mind to achieve a state of tranquility. Meditation, which could come in the form of a yoga or simple deep-breathing exercises, enhances the connection of your mind, body and soul by helping you focus on your breath and position. With each position that you assume and each breath that you take, you are allowing your mind to control your body and your soul to be revitalized.

As you become aware of each breathing cycle, the depth of your inhalation and the speed of your exhalation, you are not only letting your mind relax, but you are also allowing your body to regain its strength. Now with a clearer mind and a stronger body, you are more capable of self-control. With a stronger tie between your mind, body, and soul, you become well aware of your actions, your desires and your needs. You act according to what is right, you fulfill your needs and you eventually achieve what you have been dreaming of.

Meditate in a quiet, well-ventilated, and clean room. The room that you are going to use must be free of clutter. You can start meditating by focusing on one object in the room. It could be a flower, a painting or the window. As you focus your attention to this object, clear your mind off stressful thoughts. Then slowly shift your focus from this object to your breathing and position. Be aware of how your diaphragm contracts when you inhale and how your chest recoils when you exhale. Take note of your posture as well. Try to change your position and maintain your balance.

2. Pause

When life is getting hard on you, you stop listening to the voice inside you and you start losing your focus.

Your mind becomes clouded with so many thoughts and your soul loses its direction. When this happens, take a pause and give yourself a moment of silence. Close your eyes, take a deep breath, and stay still. Let your mind, body and soul reconnect by taking a day off and letting go of your worries and stressors for a day. Be aware of your thoughts and of the changes in your body and take a retreat. Take a moment to understand what is going on with your life right now. Is it going the way you want it to be or is there something that you need to iron out?

3. Appreciate life and Be grateful

When your mind loses its connection with your body and soul, you start to think negatively, work aimlessly and lose your motivation to live. Reconcile your mind, body and soul by starting to count your blessings today, by greeting the world with a smile upon waking up in the morning, and by being thankful for all the good and the bad moments in your life. Instead of thinking of the failures that you have had in the past, think of how you can use these opportunities to recover and succeed.

Steps to Success Action Plan

Steps to Success has been put together to give you somewhere to start on getting your Ultimate life by developing your mind, body and spirit connection!

To really have success, you may need to use this action plan a few times and trial a few different things to get the result you're after. Test, Measure and Monitor needs to become your motto until you are feeling whole inside.

Step 1-.Keep your mind, body and soul healthy- Before you can work on the whole you, you have to keep the different parts of you healthy.

Step 2-Understand that your mind, body and soul function as one- You cannot compartmentalize your health. The mind, body, and soul are all part of an intermingling force.

Step 3 –Recognize what is wrong with your life right now- It's like the old saying goes: "The first step to recovery is to admit something is wrong."

Step 4- Clear your mind and plan on how you can get over it- It's easy to become overloaded by all kinds of things, but clearing your mind will help give you a sense of peace and direction.

Step 5- Nurture wisdom- Feed your head with good things and good things will come of it.

Step 6- Execute your plans- It's not enough just to plan, you have to execute that plan!

Step 7- Reflect on your experiences and reconnect your mind, body and soul- Once you have made steps towards recovery, it's good to sometimes look back and see how far you've come! It can be a great motivating tool to see where you were before and where you are now.

Conclusion

Thank you again for buying this book!

I hope this book was able to help you to fully understand what is holding you back from being your ultimate version of you. Connecting your mind, body and spirit helps you to live in harmony with yourself, and gives you a sense of oneness, with no conflict.

The next step is to put this knowledge to good use and attempt to get the mind body spirit connection you have always dreamed off, and you are off to a flying start by reading this book and taking advantage of the Action Plan included.

Finally, if you enjoyed this book, please take the time to share your thoughts and post a review on Amazon. It'd be greatly appreciated!

Thank you and good luck!

Other Books you may be interested in...

Below you'll find some of my other books currently available through Amazon. Healthy Body Books now has over 30 books in the series, so jump on line and check them out today!

Weight Loss Motivation Unlocked: Key Strategies to Getting and Staying Motivated in 5minutes!

Exercise for Weight loss: 50 Tips to a Happier, Healthier You!

The Ultimate Guide to Being Fit for Life: Take Control of your Body and Transform your Life!

The Beginners Guide to Alternative Therapies: The Top 10 Types of Alternative Therapies Explained!

You can simply search for these amazing titles on the Amazon website.

Free Gift

Thank you again for grabbing yourself a copy of this Book Mind, Body, Spirit: The Ultimate Guide to Creating a Strong Mind, Body, Spirit Connection

I'd like to reward you with this by offering you free access to my newsletter!

You will be getting up to date information on health, fitness and diet, and also get access to getting other Healthy Body Books for free. By joining my newsletter you will be taking a big step forward in being your Healthiest Body yet!

Just visit http://www.healthybodybooks.com and get free instant access to the Healthy Body Books newsletter today!

Lastly once you finish reading this book would please review this book on Amazon. With your feedback I continue to make this book better and better.

Thank you!

Printed in Great Britain
by Amazon